Contents

Introduction

Do you need a book that helps students master the skills of proofreading? To find out if you are ready for *More Proofreading Practice, Please!* take this handy quiz:

1. My students typically proofread their work

   (A) sometimes

   (B) only on weekends

   (C) when pigs have wings

   (D) Are you kidding?

2. Proofreading is an important part of the writing process and provides students with

   (A) 12 vitamins and minerals

   (B) a whole new outlook on the world

   (C) an excuse for why their writing needs help

   (D) Are you kidding?

3. A proofreading error was the cause of

   (A) the War of 1812

   (B) the stock market crash of 1929

   (C) reality TV

   (D) Are you kidding?

Scoring

If you answered D. *Are you kidding?* to all of the above, you're ready for *More Proofreading Practice, Please!* In fact, if you didn't answer *D* above, you're also ready for the book. In general, you need *More Proofreading Practice, Please!* if:

- your students have never heard of proofreading.

- your students have heard of proofreading, but would rather shovel out horse stables with a grapefruit spoon than take the time to proofread their work.

- your students prefer stories, poems, articles, and essays that are engaging, fun, and delightful rather than tedious, dull, and pointless.

- your students like to laugh while they're learning and learn while they're laughing.

- your students need to practice proofreading and editing skills that include punctuation, capitalization, spelling, and grammar skills.

Scholastic Professional Books *More Proofreading Practice, Please! Grade 4*

More Proofreading Practice, Please!

Grade 4

by Dan Greenberg

SCHOLASTIC
PROFESSIONAL BOOKS

New York • Toronto • London • Auckland • Sydney
Mexico City • New Delhi • Hong Kong • Buenos Aires

Cover design by Gerard Fuchs
Cover illustration by Larry Jones
Interior design by Creative Pages, Inc.
Interior illustrations by Mike Moran

ISBN 0-439-18840-7

Copyright © 2003 by Dan Greenberg. All rights reserved.
Printed in the U.S.A.
1 2 3 4 5 6 7 8 9 10   40   10 09 08 07 06 05 04 03

How to Use This Book

The book is organized into four proofreading subject areas: Spelling, Punctuation and Capitalization, Grammar, and Mixed Errors. Each section includes nine activities.

The Spelling section includes topics such as plurals and homophones. Within the Punctuation and Capitalization section, topics such as proper nouns, possessives, contractions, and comma usage are covered. The Grammar section covers subject-verb agreement, tenses, sentence fragments, and more. The final section invites students to make corrections in all major categories, testing their mastery of proofreading rules.

Selections—in the form of stories, essays, poems, ads, forms, brochures, editorials, diaries, and so on—are presented in a way that allows students to make proofreading corrections right on the page using proofreading symbols. (A reproducible page of common proofreading symbols is provided on page 6.) Be sure to go over how to use these symbols. Annotated answers to each exercise are given at the end of the book.

Classroom Management

Selections in this book can be:

• distributed and completed on an individual basis.

• done as a class with you eliciting volunteer responses.

• assigned as work for partners or small cooperative groups to complete.

• distributed for homework or in-class work.

• completed as part of a Writing Program or Writing Lab.

• incorporated as part of a Five-Step Writing Process program that includes Prewriting, Drafting, Revising, Proofreading, and Publishing.

You might also try:

• having students trade writing samples and proofread each other's work.

• having students proofread papers that they have written for other subjects, such as social studies, science, or math.

• playing a proofreading game in which students are challenged to find, for example, "all 27 errors in this article."

Going Beyond

The true test of proofreading exercises is whether they carry over into students' own writing. To find out, ask students to write their own selections (based on selections in this book!) and proofread them. Stress that proofreading should include not only correcting errors, but also paying attention to the content and structure of the writing and making sure that all ideas are expressed as clearly and succinctly as possible.

Most of All

Try to make proofreading a fun part of the writing process that students look forward to doing, rather than a chore that hangs over their heads. Point out that the selections in this book become clearer, and thus more interesting, engaging, and *funny* only after they are proofread and minor errors are eliminated.

Scholastic Professional Books *More Proofreading Practice, Please! Grade 4*

5

Proofreading Symbols

a ~~big~~ dog	╲ Delete (Take it away forever!)
dig ~~dug~~ ∧	⌐ Delete and change to something else
¶ Once upon a time	¶ Begin a new paragraph
ⓛⓒ I Ḻove socks	ⓛⓒ Lowercase that capital letter
ⓒⓐⓟ in miami, Florida ≡	ⓒⓐⓟ Capitalize that lowercase letter
Ames⌄ Iowa	⌄ Insert comma
⌄⌄What's up?⌄⌄ Fred asked.	⌄⌄ ⌄⌄ Insert quotation marks
The cat sat on the mat⌄	⊙ Insert period
What time is it⌄	? Insert question mark
The ⌒dog⌒ adorable wagged its tail.	∿ Transpose (or trade positions)

Scholastic Professional Books *More Proofreading Practice, Please! Grade 4*

Name _____ Date _____

Opinion Poll

Find and mark the ten spelling errors.

The following are the results of a scientific opinion poll. Won hundred students just like yourself were asked a series of questions. Youw'll be surprised by the results!

General Questions

Number of students who

think air is a good thing to brethe **100%**

like nickeles better than quarters **0%**

are older than they were one yeer ago **99%**

Personal Questions

Number of students who

wear their socks on their ears **1%**

wear their socks over their shoeies **1%**

injoy getting a case of poison ivy **0%**

Special Duck Questions

Number of students who

think *duck* is a bird **90%**

think *duck* is something you do to get out of the way ..**5%**

think *duck* is a kind of goose **1%**

Final Questions

Number of students who

don'ot like questions **99%**

wouldn't answer are questions **98%**

wouldn't answer our questions even if we pade them ..**4%**

Name _____ Date _____

Punctuation Poem

Find and mark the ten spelling errors.

Punctuashun

Can be key

When youre writing

Poetry.

Every line will tern

Out better

When it begins

With a capital letter.

Interruptions?

They're just fine,

Insert a comma on the line.

Now here'is something

Dear to me,

I call it the

Apostrophe.

Do some questiones

Lose their spark

When you forget

A question mark?

Now wer're going;

Really rolling;

Don't forget

The semi-colon.

Try these:

Collons and quotations.

This mark's good for

Exclamaytions!

(Did I for get

Both of these?

They call them the

Parentheses.)

Well! That's all

The time I'ave got.

I'll end this poem

With a dot.

Period.

Scholastic Professional Books *More Proofreading Practice, Please! Grade 4*

Name _____ Date _____

Want Ads

Find and mark the ten spelling errors.

For Rent

Do you need someone to bark at strangers who come to your door? Rent my dog. He barks so much it'is driving me crazy! 555-1239.

Help Wanted

I have a good job for a yung person who is responsible and knows how to sharpen pencils. I have a lot of pencils and I expeck you to keep them sharp. If you don't keep them sharp I'll make you wash the dishes and clean out my garadge. Don't get me mad! Call 555-2770.

For Sale

Lite bulb, slightly used. Will fit into any socket! Runs on standard electric current. Classic bulb shape, with frosted exterior. Used only at night, by nice family who never pulled switches fast. By it for 4¢ or less. Call 555-4451.

Bicycle

Broken weels, no handlebars, no seat, spokes are broken to. It's rustie, and it never was a good bike to begin with. You can buy it for $1. Call Jake at 555-2139.

Junk!

I have a basement that is filled with mountins of junk! If you clean it out you can have everything that's in there! Everything! I'm not kidding! Call 555-2057.

Scholastic Professional Books *More Proofreading Practice, Please! Grade 4*

9

Name _____ Date _____

Weather Report

Find and mark the ten spelling errors.

The five-day forecast is given below.

Today High: 46 Low: 44		Partly Cloudy Some sun in the morning. Clouds move in the aftrenoon. Look for a sprinkle tonight.
Tomorrow High: 73 Low: 62		Showers and Thunderstorms Downpores could be heavy at times. Dangerous lightning and hale are possible. Wear your waterrproof clothes!
Tuesday High: 59 Low: 39		Rain Ending A cold front moves through on Tuseday. Look for light winds and clearing skyes.
Wednesday High: 99 Low: 79		Sunny and Hot Hie pressure brings scorching temperatures. Stay inside and drink sumthing with an ice cube in it.
Thursday High: 39 Low: 19		Mostly Sunny and Cold Winter conditions return. Close your windowes and wear a hat. Don't go out unless you have a good reson.

Scholastic Professional Books *More Proofreading Practice, Please! Grade 4*

Name _____ Date _____

Lonesome Bob's Restaurant: The Menu

Find and mark the ten spelling errors.

Appetizers

Hot Air Puffs We take the fineest quality air, scrub it until it's squeaky clean, filter it, and stir in herbs and spices. Then we deep fry it in penut oil and serve it up hot and tasty. Wow, that's good hot air!   **$4.95**

Goat Soup Goats eat grass, weeds, rubber bands—just about *anything*. We combine these ingredients—and more—to make this sup. It tastes just the way you'd expect: like something a goat would eat!   **$6.95**

Main Dishes

Crumb Balls You won't believe our crumm balls. We don't believe them ourselfs! That's why we had them tested by Hall of Fame golfer Gummy Watson. Old Gummy put a crumb ball on a tee and smacked it over 275 yards. Now that's a tasty crumb ball!   **$10.95**

Mineral Tacos We take a fresh corn tortilla, smother it in lime juice, then pour on a hole bucket of pebbles. It's a crunchy treat that's truly fit for a king or a queen!   **$12.95**

Desserts

Big Mound of Sugar It's just what we say it is. We dump a big mound of sugar in a boll. That's it. Nothing fancy. Nothing compicated. Why bother with food?   **$6.95**

Pocket Bars We leave chocolate bars in the back pockets of our pants. Then we put the pants threw the washer and the dryer. Then we peel each chocolate bar off the pocket. Wow, that's good!   **2 for $3.95**

Scholastic Professional Books *More Proofreading Practice, Please! Grade 4*

11

Name _____ Date _____

Cooking With Louie

Recipes From a Dog Who Will Eat Anything!

Find and mark the ten spelling errors.

This marvelous recipe I discoverred while traveling last summer. I call it …

Pellets Louie

1. Find a bag of dog pellets.
2. Nock the bag over.
3. Don't bother prepareing them in any way. Just spill them on the floor and eat them.

Are you on a diet? Here's a great low-fat recipe. I call it …

Wrappers Louie

1. Find an old fast-food wrapper that had a taco or berger on it.
2. Choo the wrapper.
3. Spit out the paper afterward. Stay slim on this fabulous food plan!

I learned this recipe when someone accidentale left a bag of garbage out. The eroma was amazing! I call it …

Garbage Louie

1. Find a bag of garbage.
2. Poke a hole in the bag with your teeth.
3. Eat.

Some of the best recipes can get you in real troubel. I tryed this one last summer on a picnic and was chased for it. But, it was good! I call it …

Up-On-the-Table Louie

1. Hang around while people are cooking dinner.
2. Wait until no one is looking.
3. Jump up on the table and try to eat whatever you can get.
4. Be perpared to run fast!

Scholastic Professional Books *More Proofreading Practice, Please! Grade 4*

Name _____ Date _____

You-Gene Smedley, Wrap Star

Find and mark the ten spelling errors.

My name is Smedley,

Better none as You-Gene.

I'am a wrapping fellow.

I'm a wrapping machine!

I wrapped a submarine sand witch

To eat for later.

Then tossed the hole thing in the

Refrigerator.

I wraped a birthday gift

For my coussin Betty.

I wrapped a cotton sweater.

I wrapped a box of spaghetti.

I wrapped a ball pont pen

With some cellophane tape.

I wrapped a potato, a tomato

And a seedleses grape …

Oh wait, what's that

You say about rapping?

I've got it all rong?

Now, how could this happen?

Am I not a "Wrap" Star?

Are you calling me fake?

Whoops! Now I get it. Sorey,

My mistake!

Scholastic Professional Books *More Proofreading Practice, Please! Grade 4*

13

Name _____ Date _____

Spoiled Rotten!

The Catalog for the Kid Who Has Everything!

Find and mark the ten spelling errors.

Pillow Culer

- Liquid nitrogen 980,000 BTU cooling system cools pillows fast
- Settings include *Cool, Frosty, Icy, Stone-cold Frozun*
- Never need to turn your pillow over again

Button Pusher

- Too laizy to push buttons? Get the button pusher!
- Real human beings who work by the week, day, hour, or minnute
- They work hard so you can be lazy!

Pet Space Launcher

- Real solud fuel NASA booster system
- Just like the ones used in the space shuttel
- 18 million pounds of thrust. It really orbits Earth.
- Includes tiny astronaut suits for your dog, cat, bird, or mowse
- Give pooch or kitty the vacatiun of a lifetime!

Twenty Dollar Bills

- Made of sterdy green paper
- U.S. government issue
- Good for wiping up messes, writing notes, or buying things
- Fits easily in your pocket or perse

Name _____ Date _____

New Remote Control Devices

Find and mark the ten spelling errors.

Remote Control Neihbor Changer

Push the button. Your neighbores change into different people. Also works
on people sitting next to you in school, on a bus, or in a restaurant.

Long Distanse Remote Stereo Controller

Controls stereo settings for up to 500 miles. From your oan living room, you
can turn on music for someone in Pittsburgh!

Remote Control Eye Opener

Two tired to open your eyes in the morning? No problem. Just point and clik.
Your eyes will open like a camera shutter. It will close eyes, too. Grate for sleep overs.

Remote Remote

Too tyred to push buttons? You can use this remote remote to control your other
remote from acrost the room. Come to think of it, you might as well use the remote
itself. But then, there wouldn'nt be any need for this product!

Scholastic Professional Books *More Proofreading Practice, Please! Grade 4*

15

Name _____ Date _____

How to Operate Your New Wungle CV-502 DVD Player

Find and mark the ten punctuation and capitalization errors.

Congratulations! you are now the proud new owner of a wungle CV-502. Your machine includes the latest power skip technology. Use the following instructions to access all of the special features.

Commercial Skip

This skips the commercials in any program taped. Push the red Power Skip button once?

Bore Skip

To skip dull or boring parts in programs. push the red Power Skip button twice.

Mush Skip

Do you hate those mushy parts in movies with all of that kissing! Skip over them with Mush Skip. To operate, push the red Power Skip button three times.

Good Part Replay

Your Wungle CV-502 finds good parts in movies or taped programs, and automatically replays them, whether you want, to see them or not!

Whole Movie Skip

Suppose you've chosen a Movie that has no good parts at all. Your Wungle CV-502 will automatically skip the entire movie and move on to something more interesting

Do Something Else

The Wungle CV-502 can sense when you've already watched too much tv. At this point, it automatically turns itself off and flashes this message on the screen: **Go outside and do something else!**

Scholastic Professional Books *More Proofreading Practice, Please! Grade 4*

Name _____ Date _____

Dr. Lorna, Pet Psychologist

Find and mark the ten punctuation and capitalization errors.

909 West Northern Avenue
San Diego, ca 92109
july 27, 2002
Dear Dr. Lorna
   My dog thinks he's a rooster.
Every morning he gets up and
cock-a-doodles at the sun. Then
he tries to peck. What should I do!
   Your friend,
   Chicken Dog

Dear Chick,
   Send for my new book, *How to Help Your Dog Be a Dog.* It contains tips for how to control clucking, pecking, and other chicken-like behaviors? Good cluck, I mean, luck!
Yours truly,
Dr. Lorna

4200 Beachfront Lane
St. petersburg, FL 33713
November 2, 2001
Dear Dr Lorna,
   My pet mouse is shy. I had a
party for her and she wouldn't
even come out of her hole to meet
the guests. What should I do?
Yours truly

Mouse Mom

dear Mouse,
   Is there any chance that some
of your guests were cats? Mice are
known to be shy around cats. Try
having the party again. Only this
time, don't invite any cats.
Yours truly:
Dr. Lorna

Scholastic Professional Books More Proofreading Practice, Please! Grade 4

17

Name _____ Date _____

Brush With Fame

by Sabrina Johnson

Find and mark the ten punctuation and capitalization errors.

Hollywood, May 1—I was walking my neighbor's dog when I saw another dog nearby. It was a Dalmatian. I remembered reading about the movie star tom Jangles in *Movie teen* magazine. The article said that Tom has a Dalmatian!

So, then I looked up. The guy walking the dog looked exactly like TOm Jangles!

Except, he was much younger He was also quite a bit heavier, a lot shorter, and had a beard. (I figured that this was just his disguise!)

Otherwise, he looked exactly like Tom Jangles!

So I said, Hey, Tom!" in a very friendly voice.

He said, What are you talking about? My name is Walter.

But I could tell he was just pretending. I'm sure it was so no one would recognize him?

Later, when I got home and looked at *Movie Teen* magazine, it said that the real Tom Jangles has a boxer for a dog, not a Dalmatian?

Then I thought, "Isn't that perfect. Tom even disguises his dog!

Scholastic Professional Books *More Proofreading Practice, Please! Grade 4*

Name _____ Date _____

Bad Investments

Find and mark the ten punctuation and capitalization errors.

We recommend that you *not* put your money into the following businesses.

Greasie's Restaurant

Do you like greasy food! Then Greasie's is the place for you. We fry all our food in 100% greasy oil. even the desserts are fried. Greasie's is a slippery experience!

Cheapo Inn Motels

Where else can you get a room for less than $7,00 a night? Cheapo's is the motel chain that offers no Room Service, no elevator, no beds, no televisions, no bathrooms, and no windows. You can't find a cheaper motel!

Mini Bowl

Do you like miniature golf? Then come down to the Mini bowl. It has a tiny ball, a tiny bowling lane, and even a tiny scorecard. The bowling pins are no bigger than an aspirin bottle Just try putting your fingers in the Bowling ball holes!

Doggie Wash

Do you like giving your dog a bath? If not, go to doggie Wash, the world's only automatic dog washing system. It works just like a car wash. Just strap your dog in and watch it go down the Conveyor belt. You'll never have a cleaner (or more terrified) dog!

Scholastic Professional Books *More Proofreading Practice, Please! Grade 4*

19

Name _____ Date _____

The Great Debate: Cats vs. Dogs

Find and mark the ten punctuation and capitalization errors.

Moderator: Welcome to "The Great Debate."
Our experts are here to discuss
the Pros and Cons of cats and
dogs. Cats are represented
by Zippy. Woofie, a Dog, is
representing the opposing
side. Zippy please make your
opening statement.

Zippy: First, I'd like to thank you
for asking me here. Next, I
think dogs are loud dirty,
and dim-witted.

Moderator: Woofie, will you make your opening statement.

Woofie: I would like to thank "The Great Debate" for sponsoring this
discussion. First, Zippy is wrong. Dogs are friendly, warm, and smart.

Zippy: I, disagree. If dogs are friendly, why doesn't Woofie agree with me?

Woofie: I'm not agreeing with you because you're wrong. Dogs are good.
Cats are bad.

Zippy: Can you prove your statement.

Woofie: The Dog Institute recently did a study and found that cats are sneaky,
mean, and nasty.

Zippy: That's not true!

Woofie: Yes, it is!

Zippy: No it's not!

Moderator: Ladies and gentlemen, we must interrupt this debate. Our debaters
are chasing each other around the stage. Please join us next time
when we present "Squid vs. Whale: Who's Better?

Scholastic Professional Books *More Proofreading Practice, Please! Grade 4*

Name _____ Date _____

Olympic Events for Really Lazy People

Find and mark the ten punctuation and capitalization errors.

Sleep Pentathlon

Athletes test their sleeping skills in five different areas: The Doze, The Cat-Nap, The Slumber, The snooze, and finally, The Siesta.

Just sit there

Athletes sit in chairs and do nothing. The first one, that does something loses.

Daydreaming

Athletes Imagine that they are running swimming jumping, or diving. Of course, they're only daydreaming. In reality, they're just lounging around.

The Twiddle

Athletes compete in thumb twiddling, finger twiddling, and toe twiddling. The Finalists then face each other in a twiddle-off.

Talking on the Phone in Your Pajamas and doodling

Athletes compete to see who can talk on the phone the longest while doodling? Scores will be based on doodles, time spent talking, and quality of pajamas.

Scholastic Professional Books More Proofreading Practice, Please! Grade 4

21

Name _____ Date _____

Making Time to Be Silly in a Busy World

Find and mark the ten punctuation and capitalization errors.

Silliness is on the rise. Active people find that being silly fits today's more active lifestyle. Listen to what these people are saying about finding time to be silly.

Stockbroker Maggie W. said "I take time to be silly every day. After a hard day I like to make goofy faces in the mirror. It's great!

"School is hard," said Chuck C., fourth-grader: "Being silly helps. I put a piece of cheese on my Nose. Then I feel great. Being silly is the best!"

Mona T., mom, claims, It's important for my kids to learn to be silly when they're young. I want them to be bungling, ridiculous, and doofy. It will help them when they grow up"

It's hard to find time to act like a fool when you're an important lawyer" explains Bonnie B "Sometimes during a meeting, I just put my dog on my head and juggle like a clown. Then I take the dog off and, continue talking to my client."

Scholastic Professional Books More Proofreading Practice, Please! Grade 4

Name _____ Date _____

Consumer Tips: How to Make Gum Last Longer

Find and mark the ten punctuation and capitalization errors.

How do I make my gum last longer? That is one of the most frequently asked questions we hear at Consumer Headquarters. After careful study, we've come up with the following helpful tips?

1. Don't chew so much. Studies show that chewing reduces Flavor. The more you chew, the more Flavor you lose. So try to not chew so much. Just put the gum in your mouth hold it, and chew once every 60 seconds.

2. Don't chew so hard. Chewing hard reduces flavor. So chew more softly. Imagine you are chewing a tiny robins egg. Remember that if you chew too hard, you'll break the egg

3. Take the gum out of your mouth. Spit the gum out in your hand and roll it into a long-lasting ball To make it last forever, donate it to the Museum of Gum.

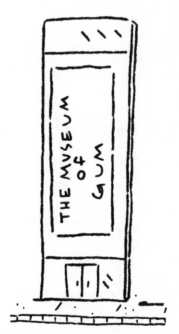

4. Don't take the gum out of the pack. Gum flavor will last for month's if you simply leave it wrapped up in the pack. This is for people who really want long-lasting gum:

5. Don't even buy the gum in the first place. Studies show that the longest-lasting gum of all is gum that you don't buy. After all, if you don't have any gum, how can it lose flavor.

Scholastic Professional Books *More Proofreading Practice, Please! Grade 4*

23

Name _____ Date _____

What They Do on Their Day Off

Find and mark the ten punctuation and capitalization errors.

An interviewed dog said. "By the time I get my day off I'm really exhausted from barking and sniffing all week. I don't bark a bit. If I need to speak, I meow softly. I don't wag my tail, except for emergencies. I lie around and read the newspaper.

Arnie, the couch potato, said, "sitting around watching mindless TV all week is a tough job. On my day off; I avoid television as much as possible. I go to museums. I read a lot. I try to stay away from couches."

A phone interview with a Woman who makes those annoying phone calls selling things revealed, 'I love my job. How many people can say that. So on my day off, I spend the day on the phone. I call strangers and ask them if they'd like to change their long distance company. I do this for nothing. That's how much I love my job!"

In the barnyard, a chicken said, do you know how hard it is to lay an egg every day? On my day off, I like to go horseback riding. Did you say you've never seen a chicken riding a horse. Look around, especially on Tuesdays. A lot of chickens take Tuesdays off for a trail ride."

Name _____ Date _____

The Big Interview

This week Jerry Jones interviews Coach Bobbie Tantrum, Uptown School dodge ball coach.

Find and mark the ten grammar errors.

Jerry: Welcome to the shows, Ms. Tantrum.

Bobbie: I'd like to say right off that I'm hot under the collar! I'd like to say right off that I'm steaming mad!

Jerry: Why is that?

Bobbie: They is throwing the ball right at my team!

Jerry: Who, Ms. Tantrum? Who's throwing right at you?

Bobbie: The other team! The other team throwing the ball at my team. It isn't right. I'm going to take it anymore!

Jerry: But, coach, this is dodge ball. The point of dodge ball is to throw the ball at the other team.

Bobbie: It is? Who told you that?

Jerry: It's common knowledge!

Bobbie: Really? No wonder my team never wins.

Jerry: I think that your player Tonya Lightoff has a good arm. Is her your best player?

Bobbie: I guess she can throw hardest than Star Renite. If we play by your rules, Tonya could be the star. His arm is strong.

Jerry: What's your game plan, coach?

Bobbie: I think it's time to stop talking and start coaching this team.

Jerry: Thanks, Ms. Tantrum. That were Bobbie Tantrum, coach of the Uptown School dodge ball team. Good night, fans.

Scholastic Professional Books More Proofreading Practice, Please! Grade 4

25

Name _____ Date _____

My Most Embarrassing Moment

Find and mark the ten grammar errors.

Dinah Bingle, Member of Congress, said, "I was giving a speech to the members' of the Askalooska Polar Bear Club. Suddenly, I realized that I didn't have any idea what I was talking about! I didn't let that stop me. In fact, I've gone on to become a successful lawmaker. Of course, I still have no idea what I be talking about."

Fred Yerkle, Rude Cab Driver, explained, "I was driving down the street. Suddenly, I noticed that I wasn't snarling and I noticed that I wasn't being rude. I wasn't changing lanes, tailgating, or hogging the road. I was just driving. I was so embarrassed! Quickly, I went back to my old self and honked at a truck. I felt much more better."

Johnny Pilson, Fourth Grader, said, "I was doing my homework when I realized that the assignment were fun. I didn't told anyone. I thought the feeling would go away. But, it's still here. I actually enjoy doing my homework."

Louie, a Dog, laughed, "A human spilled something under the table. I think it was a French fry. I didn't run to get it! I don't know what came over me. Maybe it had something to do with that seven-pound turkey leg that I'd just finish eating. Whatever it was, I'm better now. When something spills from the table, I zip over there and grab it!"

Scholastic Professional Books *More Proofreading Practice, Please! Grade 4*

Name _____ Date _____

Spelling Tips From Mr. Mickey

Find and mark the ten grammar errors.

Tip 1

Some spelling mistakes is actually correct. For example, the word *wrong* often is spelled wrong. Of course, this be wrong. But it's not a mistake. It's just wrong.

Tip 2

Persons often spell words incorrectly when you ask them to lend you money. When they mean to say "yes" they spell their answers "no."

Tip 3

Big words can be tricky. For example, looks at the word *smiles*. Though she may not seem big, there is a mile between the first and last letters of the word.

Tip 4

What's the harder word to spell? That would be *diamond*. A diamond is 13 times harder than steel, and 96 times harder than oatmeal.

The following are general tip to improve your spelling.

1. Never spell on a empty stomach.
2. When spelling dangerous words, always wore a helmet and goggles.
3. Wash all dirty words with soap and water before spell.

Scholastic Professional Books *More Proofreading Practice, Please! Grade 4*

27

Name _____ Date _____

The Coming Biscuit Crisis

Will we have enough biscuits for the 21st century?

Find and mark the ten grammar errors.

The Situation Right Now

At the moment, the biscuit supply holding up. But, biscuits are disappearing at an alarming rate. If this trend keeps up, we be completely out of biscuits by the year 2028.

Every day, thousands of biscuit are left uneaten, destroyed, or threw away. Don't let this happen to your biscuits!

Trends

Some people seem to think the biscuit supply be endless. It ain't. Remember, once you eat a biscuit, it's gone.

Organizations

Groups like S.O.B. (Save Our Biscuits) are organizing. They use rallies and concerts to got the word out. Slowly, minds is being changed. People are becoming aware of the Great Biscuit Shortage.

What You Can Do

• Save your biscuits!

• Tell them friends and neighbors to recycle biscuits.

• Organize a Biscuit Day for yours school.

28

Scholastic Professional Books *More Proofreading Practice, Please! Grade 4*

Name _____ Date _____

How I Invented the Amazing Spaghetti Gutter

by Sandy Beech

Find and mark the ten grammar errors.

Take a look at the first picture. That's I, Sandy Beech, after eating a bowl of spaghetti.

I loves spaghetti. But, spaghetti is a mess! That's why I invent the Amazing Spaghetti Gutter. The Amazing Spaghetti Gutter have patented Total Surround® technology. It works like the cow-catcher on a railroad train to whisk away spills before they pile up!

Take a look at me after I use the Amazing Spaghetti Gutter. I just has a big bowl of spaghetti and you can't even tell! My blouses is clean. My chin is dry. The Amazing Spaghetti Gutter sucked up the spills before they even started!

How much would you pay for a 100% all-vinyl Spaghetti Gutter? Millions has been sold for $695.95.

But today, in this limited offer, you can order a Amazing Spaghetti Gutter for only $19.95! That's right! You get the Gutter, attachments, instruction booklet, and video all for only $19.95!

Bonus! If you order today, get 50 foot of extra-heavy duty garden hose for rinsing after a big meal. It's absolutely free!

Name _____ Date _____

How to Become a Millionaire Before the Age of 12

Find and mark the ten grammar errors.

Would you like to be a millionaire before you're twelve? Others have done it. You can do it, to. Just follow these helpful pointers.

Step 1 Get to know someone who has several million dollar and want to give some of it away.

Step 2 Ask that person to gave you a million dollars. Remember to say, "Please!"

Step 3 If the person don't give you the money, say, "Pretty please with a cherry on top." This usual works. If it doesn't work, go to step 4.

Step 4 Beg and whine. If this don't work, go to step 5.

Step 5 Keep your eyes open for the following:

$ Rare coins that be worth an million dollars

$ Buried treasure

$ Big bags of gold

$ Lost art masterpieces

$ Big bags of diamonds

Step 6 If all else fails, become a superstar actor, singer, or athlete. Or, you can just look around for an big bag stuffed with money.

Scholastic Professional Books *More Proofreading Practice, Please! Grade 4*

Name _____ Date _____

Louie's Doggy Dictionary

Find and mark the ten grammar errors.

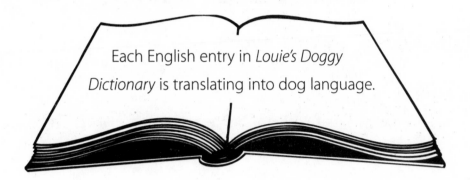

Each English entry in *Louie's Doggy Dictionary* is translating into dog language.

ball (bawl) *noun* This is the round thing that you chase. Then, you got food.

down (doun) *verb* This is something that people yell at you. When you hear it, you should jump up several times, then stopped. If you don't get any food, try jumping again.

good boy/good girl (gud boi) (gud guhrl) *noun* This means not nothing. It's just something that they say to you before they give you food.

happy (hap • ee) *noun* I not sure what this word means. I know it have something to do with food.

hello (hel • oh) *noun* This am a word that human's use when they want to give you food.

walk (wawk) *noun* This is something you does around the block before you go homes to get food.

Name _____ Date _____

Beyond the Microwave

New Inventions That Take Microwave Technology to the Next Level

Find and mark the ten grammar errors.

The Cold Wave

Old-fashioned microwaves make things hot. The Cold Wave makes things cold. Put a spoonful of water in the Cold Wave for 30 seconds and out comes a ice cube!

The Flavor Wave

Suppose you has a bowl of tasteless mush. Put it in the Flavor Wave for two minutes and it'll bursting with fresh flavor! Leave it in for three minutes and it'll taste like a gourmet meal from an fancy restaurant!

The Reconstituter

Put a chocolate cake in the Reconstituter for six minutes. Soon you got the ingredients that made the cake: flours, sugar, eggs, chocolate, and milk. How do this work? We have no idea!

The "Stale-erator"

Does you like leftovers? Put fresh food in the "Stale-erator" and turn it on. Soon, it taste four days old! This thing make food so stale no one will want to eat it!

Scholastic Professional Books *More Proofreading Practice, Please! Grade 4*

Name _____ Date _____

Build a Better Mousetrap Competition

Find and mark the ten grammar errors.

Virtual Mousetrap

Help the mouse puts on a pair of goggles. Inside the goggles, the mouse will seen a piece of virtual cheese. When the mouse lunges for the cheese, it gets catched in a virtual trap.

Advantage: No muss, no fuss.

Drawback: It works in virtual reality only. In the real world, you'll still stuck with the mouse.

Golf Vacation Get-Away Mousetrap

The mouse is lured by a lavish golf vacation offer. The offer includes transportation, hotel, and golf tiny clubs. The mouse is taken on vacation and not never comes back.

Advantage: Gets rid of the mouse for good.

Drawback: It might maybe attract some human golf fans.

Shop-Till-You-Drop Mousetrap

The mouse is lured by department store sales of up to 80% off. The mouse shop so much that you finally drops. You haul the mouse away.

Advantage: Gets rid of mouse for good.

Drawback: The mouse will be better dressed than you is.

Scholastic Professional Books *More Proofreading Practice, Please! Grade 4*

33

Name _____ Date _____

The Four Biggest Mistakes That Kids Make

Find and mark the twelve errors. They may be spelling, punctuation, capitalization, or grammar errors.

Mistake 1: Leaving a Half-Eaten Candy Bar in Your Room

You start eating a candy bar. Then you put it down. Two years later you find it. Your mom asks, What's this moldy thing? You say, "I don't know." She get mad at you. If you don't shape up, she'll grond you. You'll miss the party at Lizetts house.

Mistake 2: Not Finishing Your Homework

You start your homework. Then you get distracted. Your mom says, "Did you finish your homework." You say, "No." She threatens to ground you. You may miss the party at Lizett house.

Lizett's Having a Party!

DATE February 6

TIME 5:00 P.M.

PLACE 612 Blue St.

Mistake 3: Failing to Clean Up Your Room

You start to clean you're room. Then suddenelly you remember that you need to make a phone call. Three hours later, your mom says "Why didn't you finish cleaning your room?" You say, "I forgetted." Your mom's had enough. You're grounded. You're going to miss the party at Lizett's house.

Mistake 4: Not Remembering the Party

You've been planning for the party all week. Then you do something foolish (like failing to clean up your room). Your mom grounds you! You apologize and promise to correct your mistake. Your mom changes her mind. You hurry to Lizett's house. But you made another mistake. The party is tomorrow!

Scholastic Professional Books *More Proofreading Practice, Please! Grade 4*

Name _____ Date _____

Behind the Music

The Stories Behind the Songs You Love

Find and mark the twelve errors. They may be spelling, punctuation, capitalization, or grammar errors.

This week we interviewed Harvey Harv about its knew song, "Har dee Har."

On the melody and lyrics: Basically, there is no melody. I just hum whatever comes into my head. There are no Lyrics. I just sing whatever comes into my head. I know that it doesn't not rhyme or make much sense, but is that necessary for good music?

On those silly hand motions Harvey does when he sings: I imagine I have been tossed in a big vat of Vanilla pudding. Then I have to swim to get out. Those hand motions are the way I swim out of the puddin.

On fans: Fans are cool. I love fans. I'm one of the bigest fans of my fans. In fact, you could say my fans and I is really alike. Except I'm famous and get paid millions of dollers, and they get nothing.

On fame: I'd rather be known as a good musician than be famous. Wait a minute. No; I wouldn't.

On money: I'd rather be a good musician than have mony. Wait a minute. That's not true either. I'd rather have the money?

Scholastic Professional Books *More Proofreading Practice, Please! Grade 4*

35

Name _____ Date _____

World Records for Being Late

Find and mark the twelve errors. They may be spelling, punctuation, capitalization, or grammar errors.

Late to School

Bach Nguyen, of river city Iowa, was so late to school that by the time the third-grader showed up to class he was actually in the seveneth grade!

Late Library Book

Cicely Petzle of Springfield, Ohio was so late in returning a libary book that the library had closed, the building had been torn down, and a bozo Burger Restaurant had been built in its place. Cicely ordered a Bozo Burger and fries. Then she sat down and read her overdo book.

Late to Pick Up the Kids at Soccer practice

Sanjay Kota were so late to pick up his daughter at soccer practice that by the time he arrive his daughter had grown up, joined the Olympic soccer team, and won a medal.

Late Homework

Delia Cantu's current events homework report was so late that by the time she turned it in the subject was no longer a current event. In fact, it appeared in Delias history book in the section called "Voises of the Past."

Scholastic Professional Books More Proofreading Practice, Please! Grade 4

Name _____ Date _____

True Confession: I wore two left shoes for five years!

by Joe Drudge

Find and mark the twelve errors. They may be spelling, punctuation, capitalization, or grammar errors.

It's the truth! I did war to left shoes for five years. Well, actually it was more like two hours. But it felt like five years!

Here's how it started. I put on my left shoe. Then I put on my other shoe. And, here's the important thing, it be a second left shoe. But, I didn't notise.

At first, it feeled funny. I keeped thinking, "What's the matter with my shoe?"

Then things got serious. I went to my ballroom danceing class at Hank's house of Dance. My partner, Wanda, said, Joey, you dance like you've got two left feet!" I thought she was just being critical of my bad dancing. Little did I know.

Finally, we stopped dancing and sit down to get something to drink. I had a root beer. Then Wanda said, "Joey, you're wearing two left shoes"

I looked down. She was right. I was wearing two left shoes. I didn't know what to do.

Did I learn anything from this experience? Yes! Don't wear two left shoes. Don't wear two rite shoes, either. If you happen to wear two left shoes, *stay calm*. Remove the shoe from your right foot. Walk as you would normally. Wearing one left shoe is better than two.

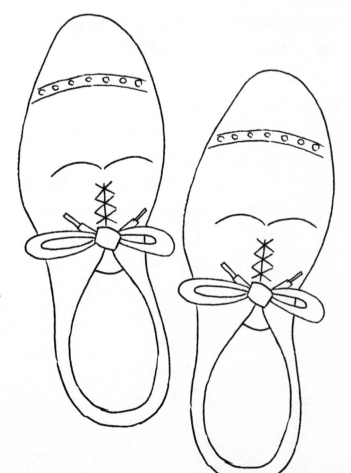

Scholastic Professional Books *More Proofreading Practice, Please! Grade 4*

37

Name _____ Date _____

Science Gab

This week's question: *Can dogs talk?*

Find and mark the twelve errors. They may be spelling, punctuation, capitalization, or grammar errors.

DR. FOBES: Hello, I'm Dr. Joann Fobes. Our special guest today on "Science Gab" Sir Anthony Elwood Burwash Wedge. Sir Anthony is a expert on dog behavior. Let's start by asking the question, "Can dogs talk. "Sir Anthony can dogs talk?

SIR ANTHONY: I'd like to begin by saying that dogs can talk. I can proov it.

DR. FOBES: How?

SIR ANTHONY: I've taken the liberty of bringing my dog rex to the program. Rex speaked to the nice woman.

REX: Rolf! Yap, yap, yap! Rolf! Yap!

SIR ANTHONY: There. Did you hear that?

DR. FOBES: What did Rex say?

SIR ANTHONY: Wasn't it obvious? He said, "Of course I can talk! Now give me a biskit!"

DR. FOBES: It don't sound like that to me. It sounds like yapping and yipping.

SIR ANTHONY: Rex, tell the man again.

REX: Yap! Rolf, rolf, rolf! Yap! Yap, yap!

SIR ANTHONY: Now, shurly you heard that?

DR. FOBES: Heard what?

SIR ANTHONY: I don't think this interview is going well at all. Rex and I are leaveing. Say good-bye, Rex!

REX: Yap, yap, yap!

Scholastic Professional Books *More Proofreading Practice, Please! Grade 4*

Name _____ Date _____

Book Ideas That Failed

Find and mark the twelve errors. They may be spelling, punctuation, capitalization, or grammar errors.

Henry the Snail, Private Detective, by Nancy Noggs

Here are the adventures of Henry the Snail, a Private eye who has one problem. He am incredibly slow! It takes him about ten minutes just to answer the phone! By the time he arives, the case has usually been solve by someone else! Henry uses his *wits* to make it as a detective.

The Whiners' Club, by Rodney Riter

This book is about a bunch of kids get together every week to complain about things. They complain about school, freinds parents, holes in their socks, you name it!

Why Is Everyone in Fourth Grade Always Looking at Me? by Alice Slack

Main character Annie Dimble go to school with a big sign on her back that says, STOP STARING AT ME! Of course, everyone stares.

Give Me Back My Ball-Point Pen, by Sonny Day

A boy lends a friend a pen The book relate the story of his eforts to get the pen back.

Why Is Fourth Grade So Difficult? by Alice Slack

This book is the sixth in the series by Alice Slack, which profiles the life of Annie Dimble. This time, Annie mistakenlly enrolls in college instead of the fourth grade. No wonder the homework is so hard!

Scholastic Professional Books *More Proofreading Practice, Please! Grade 4*

39

Name _____ Date _____

The Evening News

Featuring Richard, the Talking Cat

Find and mark the twelve errors. They may be spelling, punctuation, capitalization, or grammar errors.

"For those of you just tuning in, the evening news will now be reported by a new crack team of cat reporters. I'm Richard, and I'm a talking tabby cat. Our top story today is 'Dogs—are they just plane no good?' Recent studies have indicated that dogs are lowd, stupid, and ugly.

But, is they also no good? For more on this braking story, here's Jennifer."

"This is Jennifer the talking Siamese cat. I'm in the home of a dog named Spot. You'll notice that Spot is sleeping. Let's see what happens when I woke up Spot from his nap."

"BARK! BARK! BARK! BARK! BARK! BARK!"

"There you have it, Richard. Just as predicted, this dog was loud, stupid, and, I must say, *just plain no good!* This is Jennifer reporting live from the homes of Spot the dog."

"Thank you, Jennifer. Our next story is 'How delicious is cat food, really?' For more on our story, here's Chester."

"Hi, this is Chester the horse. I have six varietys of cat food in front of me. I tasted all of them. Richard, cat food is not delicious!"

"Thank you, Chester." I must say that I disagree with Chester here. I've ate Cat Food dozens of times before. I think it's delicious! Well, that's all the time we have now. Join me tomorrow when I'll have a special report 'Is cat nip just for cats?' Until then, good night and good mews, I mean, news."

Scholastic Professional Books *More Proofreading Practice, Please! Grade 4*

Name _____ Date _____

Urban Myths

That may or may not be true!

Find and mark the twelve errors. They may be spelling, punctuation, capitalization, or grammar errors.

Myth 1: Their are invisibel monsters that eat homework, lose things, and steal you're money.

This is absolutely true. Why hasn't anyone ever seen these monsters. You haven't not seen them because they're invisible, of course.

Myth 2: Any line you join in the supermarket will end up being the slowest line.

This seems true. But what about the other people? Wouldn't their lines also go the slowest? Doesn't that mean everyones line would be the slowest? Wait a second. Maybe it is! That explains why it takes so long to shop in the supermarket.

Myth 3: Fast food is neither fast, nor food.

If you doesn't believe it, order a bucket of chicken. You'll, see.

Myth 4: Pigeons is actually intelligent rats who has invented a way to fly.

It's possible. But if they're so intelligent, why are they always begging for food?

Myth 5: If you're nice to others, they'll be nice to you:

This has to be a myth. Hey, wait a minute. Maybe not. Maybe that's the whole problme!

Name _____ Date _____

The Proofreader

Find and mark the twelve errors. They may be spelling, punctuation, capitalization, or grammar errors.

Once there was a proofreader who was very, very lazy. he forgot capitals at the beginnings of sentences. He forgot commas periods, and other types of punctuation He even forgot to corect speling erors. Sometimes he even forgetted to fix grammar mistakes.

When people told the proofreader about his mistakes, he said, "So what? What could possibly happen from a few proofreading errors?"

One day the proofreader was proofreading a recipe for bagels. The recipe was supposed to call for 14 ounces of yeast. But the proofreader's mistake said 14 pounds of yeast.

Well, wouldn't you know it, the proofreader wandered into a bagel store next day. This was just after the bagel baker had added 14 pounds of yeast instead of 14 ounces.

"I'll have one poppy sead bagel," said the proofreader.

Suddenly, the bagels explode. The proofreader got hit by a flying bagel. In fact, it stuck to his nose!

At the hospital, the proofreader asked the doctor, "Why you laughing?"

"I'm sorry," the doctor said. "I've not never seen a bagel stuck to somebody's nose before. How did it happen?"

The proofreader told the story while the doctor extracted the bagel. Today, his nose is as good as new. He's also a much better proofreader. Now he realizes what can happen from just one small mistake.

Scholastic Professional Books *More Proofreading Practice, Please! Grade 4*

Opinion Poll, page 7

Punctuation

The following are the results of a scientific opinion poll. One hundred students just like yourself were asked a series of questions. You'll be surprised by the results!

General Questions

Number of students who

think air is a good thing to breathe	100%
like nickels better than quarters	0%
are older than they were one year ago	99%

Personal Questions

Number of students who

wear their socks on their ears	1%
wear their socks over their shoes	1%
enjoy getting a case of poison ivy	0%

Special Duck Questions

Number of students who

think *duck* is a bird	90%
think *duck* is something you do to get out of the way	5%
think *duck* is a kind of goose	1%

Final Questions

Number of students who

don't like questions	99%
wouldn't answer our questions	98%
wouldn't answer our questions even if we paid them	4%

Weather Report, page 10

The five-day forecast is given below.

Today	Partly Cloudy
	Some sun in the morning. Clouds move in the afternoon. Look for a sprinkle tonight.
High: 46	
Low: 44	
Tomorrow	Showers and Thunderstorms
	Downpours could be heavy at times. Dangerous lightning and hail are possible. Wear your waterproof clothes!
High: 73	
Low: 62	
Tuesday	Rain Ending
	A cold front moves through on Tuesday. Look for light winds and clearing skies.
High: 59	
Low: 39	
Wednesday	Sunny and Hot
	High pressure brings scorching temperatures. Stay inside and drink something with an ice cube in it.
High: 99	
Low: 79	
Thursday	Mostly Sunny and Cold
	Winter conditions return. Close your windows and wear a hat. Don't go out unless you have a good reason.
High: 39	
Low: 19	

Punctuation Poem, page 8

Punctuation

Can be key
When you're writing
Poetry.
Every line will turn
Out better
When it begins
With a capital letter.
Interruptions?
They're just fine,
Insert a comma on the line.
Now here's something
Dear to me,
I call it the
Apostrophe.
Do some questions
Lose their spark
When you forget
A question mark?

we're
Now we're going;
Really rolling;
Don't forget
The semi-colon.
Try these:
Colons and quotations.
This mark's good for
Exclamations!
(Did I forget
Both of these?
They call them the
Parentheses.)
Well! That's all
I've
The time I have got.
I'll end this poem
With a dot.
Period.

Lonesome Bob's Restaurant: The Menu, page 11

Appetizers

Hot Air Puffs We take the finest quality air, scrub it until it's squeaky clean, filter it, and stir in herbs and spices. Then we deep fry it in peanut oil and serve it up hot and tasty. Wow, that's good hot air! $4.95

Goat Soup Goats eat grass, weeds, rubber bands—just about anything. We combine these ingredients—and more—to make this soup. It tastes just the way you'd expect: like something a goat would eat! $6.95

Main Dishes

Crumb Balls You won't believe our crumb balls. We don't believe them ourselves. That's why we had them tested by Hall of Fame golfer Gummy Watson. Old Gummy put a crumb ball on a tee and smacked it over 275 yards. Now that's a tasty crumb ball! $10.95

Mineral Tacos We take a fresh corn tortilla, smother it in lime juice, then pour on a hole bucket of pebbles. It's a crunchy treat that's truly fit for a king or a queen! $12.95

Desserts

Big Mound of Sugar It's just what we say it is. We dump a big mound of sugar in a bowl. That's it. Nothing fancy. Nothing complicated. Why bother with food? $6.95

Pocket Bars We leave chocolate bars in the back pockets of our pants. Then we put the pants through the washer and the dryer. Then we peel each chocolate bar off the pocket. Wow, that's good! 2 for $3.95

Want Ads, page 9

For Rent

Do you need someone to bark at strangers who come to your door? Rent my dog. He barks so much it's driving me crazy! 555-1239.

Help Wanted

I have a good job for a young person who is responsible and knows how to sharpen pencils. I have a lot of pencils and I expect you to keep them sharp. If you don't keep them sharp, I'll make you wash the dishes and clean out my garage. Don't get me mad! Call 555-2770.

For Sale

Light bulb, slightly used. Will fit into any socket! Runs on standard electric current. Classic bulb shape, with frosted exterior. Used only at night, by nice family who never pulled switches fast. By it for 4¢ or less. Call 555-4451.

Bicycle

Broken weels, no handlebars, no seat, spokes are broken too. It's rusty, and it never was a good bike to begin with. You can buy it for $1. Call Jake at 555-2139.

Junk!

I have a basement that is filled with mountains of junk! If you clean it out you can have everything that's in there! Everything! I'm not kidding! Call 555-2057.

Cooking With Louie, page 12

This marvelous recipe I discovered while traveling last summer. I call it . . . Pellets Louie

1. Find a bag of dog pellets. 2. Knock the bag over.
3. Don't bother preparing them in any way. Just spill them on the floor and eat them.

Are you on a diet? Here's a great low-fat recipe. I call it . . . Wrappers Louie

1. Find an old fast-food wrapper that had a taco or burger on it. 2. Chew the wrapper. 3. Spit out the paper afterward. Stay slim on this fabulous food plan!

I learned this recipe when someone accidentally left a bag of garbage out. The aroma was amazing! I call it . . . Garbage Louie

1. Find a bag of garbage. 2. Poke a hole in the bag with your teeth. 3. Eat.

Some of the best recipes can get you in real trouble. I tried this one last summer on a picnic and was chased for it. But, it was good! I call it . . . Up-On-the-Table Louie

1. Hang around while people are cooking dinner.
2. Wait until no one is looking. 3. Jump up on the table and try to eat whatever you can get. 4. Be prepared to run fast!

Answer Key

You-Gene Smedley, Wrap Star, page 13

My name is Smedley,
Better known as You-Gene.
I'm a wrapping fellow.
I'm a wrapping machine!
I wrapped a submarine sandwich
To eat for later.
Then tossed the hole thing in the
Refrigerator.
I wrapped a birthday gift
For my cousin Betty.
I wrapped a cotton sweater.
I wrapped a box of spaghetti.
I wrapped a ball point pen
With some cellophane tape.
I wrapped a potato, a tomato
And a seedless grape . . .
Oh wait, what's that
You say about rapping?
I've got it all wrong?
Now, how could this happen?
Am I not a "Wrap" Star?
Are you calling me fake?
Whoops! Now I get it. Sorry,
My mistake!

How to Operate Your New Wungle CV-502 DVD Player, page 16

Congratulations! you are now the proud new owner of a wungle CV-502. Your machine includes the latest power skip technology. Use the following instructions to access all of the special features.

Commercial Skip This skips the commercials in any program taped. Push the red Power Skip button once.

Bore Skip To skip dull or boring parts in programs, push the red Power Skip button twice.

Mush Skip Do you hate those mushy parts in movies with all of that kissing? Skip over them with Mush Skip. To operate, push the red Power Skip button three times.

Good Part Replay Your Wungle CV-502 finds good parts in movies or taped programs and automatically replays them, whether you want to see them or not!

Whole Movie Skip Suppose you've chosen a Movie that has no good parts at all. Your Wungle CV-502 will automatically skip the entire movie and move on to something more interesting.

Do Something Else The Wungle CV-502 can sense when you've already watched too much tv. At this point, it automatically turns itself off and flashes this message on the screen: Go outside and do something else!

Spoiled Rotten!, page 14

Pillow Cooler
• Liquid nitrogen 980,000 BTU cooling system cools pillows fast
• Settings include Cool, Frosty, Icy, Stone-cold Frozen
• Never need to turn your pillow over again

Button Pusher
• Too lazy to push buttons? Get the button pusher!
• Real human beings who work by the week, day, hour, or minute
• They work hard so you can be lazy!

Pet Space Launcher
• Real solid fuel NASA booster system
• Just like the ones used in the space shuttle
• 18 million pounds of thrust. It really orbits Earth.
• Includes tiny astronaut suits for your dog, cat, bird, or mouse
• Give pooch or kitty the vacation of a lifetime!

Twenty Dollar Bills
• Made of sturdy green paper
• U.S. government issue
• Good for wiping up messes, writing notes, or buying things
• Fits easily in your pocket or purse

Dr. Lorna, Pet Psychologist, page 17

909 West Northern Avenue
San Diego, ca 92109
july 27, 2002
Dear Dr. Lorna,
My dog thinks he's a rooster. Every morning he gets up and cock-a-doodles at the sun. Then he tries to peck. What should I do?
Your friend, Chicken Dog

Dear Chick,
Send for my new book, How to Help Your Dog Be a Dog. It contains tips for how to control clucking, pecking, and other chicken-like behaviors. Good cluck, I mean, luck!
Yours truly, Dr. Lorna

4200 Beachfront Lane
St. petersburg, FL 33713
November 2, 2001
Dear Dr. Lorna,
My pet mouse is shy. I had a party for her and she wouldn't even come out of her hole to meet the guests. What should I do?
Yours truly, Mouse Mom

dear Mouse,
Is there any chance that some of your guests were cats? Mice are known to be shy around cats. Try having the party again. Only this time, don't invite any cats.
Yours truly, Dr. Lorna

New Remote Control Devices, page 15

Remote Control Neihbor Changer
Push the button. Your neighbors change into different people. Also works on people sitting next to you in school, on a bus, or in a restaurant.

Long Distance Remote Stereo Controller
Controls stereo settings for up to 500 miles. From your own living room, you can turn on music for someone in Pittsburgh!

Remote Control Eye Opener
Too tired to open your eyes in the morning? No problem. Just point and click. Your eyes will open like a camera shutter. It will close eyes, too. Great for sleep overs.

Remote Remote
Too tired to push buttons? You can use this remote remote to control your other remote from across the room. Come to think of it, you might as well use the remote itself. But then, there wouldn't be any need for this product!

Brush With Fame, page 18

Hollywood, May 1—I was walking my neighbor's dog when I saw another dog nearby. It was a Dalmatian. I remembered reading about the movie star tom Jangles in Movie teen magazine. The article said that Tom has a Dalmatian!

So, then I looked up. The guy walking the dog looked exactly like Tom Jangles!

Except, he was much younger. He was also quite a bit heavier, a lot shorter, and had a beard. (I figured that this was just his disguise!)

Otherwise, he looked exactly like Tom Jangles!

So I said, "Hey, Tom!" in a very friendly voice.

He said, "What are you talking about? My name is Walter."

But I could tell he was just pretending. I'm sure it was so no one would recognize him.

Later, when I got home and looked at Movie Teen magazine, it said that the real Tom Jangles has a boxer for a dog, not a Dalmatian!

Then I thought, "Isn't that perfect. Tom even disguises his dog!"

44

Bad Investments, page 19

We recommend that you *not* put your money into the following businesses.

Greasie's Restaurant

Do you like greasy food? Then Greasie's is the place for you. We fry all our food in 100% greasy oil, even the desserts are fried. Greasie's is a slippery experience!

Cheapo Inn Motels

Where else can you get a room for less than $7.00 a night? Cheapo's is the motel chain that offers no room service, no elevator, no beds, no televisions, no bathrooms, and no windows. You can't find a cheaper motel!

Mini Bowl

Do you like miniature golf? Then come down to the Mini bowl. It has a tiny ball, a tiny bowling lane, and even a tiny scorecard. The bowling pins are no bigger than an aspirin bottle. Just try putting your fingers in the bowling ball holes!

Doggie Wash

Do you like giving your dog a bath? If not, go to doggie Wash, the world's only automatic dog washing system. It works just like a car wash. Just strap your dog in and watch it go down the conveyor belt. You'll never have a cleaner (or more terrified) dog!

The Great Debate: Cats vs. Dogs, page 20

Moderator: Welcome to "The Great Debate." Our experts are here to discuss the Pros and Cons of cats and dogs. Cats are represented by Zippy. Woofie, a Dog, is representing the opposing side. Zippy, please make your opening statement.

Zippy: First, I'd like to thank you for asking me here. Next, I think dogs are loud, dirty, and dim-witted.

Moderator: Woofie, will you make your opening statement?

Woofie: I would like to thank "The Great Debate" for sponsoring this discussion. First, Zippy is wrong. Dogs are friendly, warm, and smart.

Zippy: I disagree. If dogs are friendly, why doesn't Woofie agree with me?

Woofie: I'm not agreeing with you because you're wrong. Dogs are good. Cats are bad.

Zippy: Can you prove your statement?

Woofie: The Dog Institute recently did a study and found that cats are sneaky, mean, and nasty.

Zippy: That's not true!

Woofie: Yes, it is!

Zippy: No, it's not!

Moderator: Ladies and gentlemen, we must interrupt this debate. Our debaters are chasing each other around the stage. Please join us next time when we present "Squid vs. Whale: Who's Better?"

Olympic Events for Really Lazy People, page 21

Sleep Pentathlon

Athletes test their sleeping skills in five different areas: The Doze, The Cat-Nap, The Slumber, The snooze, and finally, The Siesta.

Just sit there

Athletes sit in chairs and do nothing. The first one that does something loses.

Daydreaming

Athletes imagine that they are running, swimming, jumping, or diving. Of course, they're only daydreaming. In reality, they're just lounging around.

The Twiddle

Athletes compete in thumb twiddling, finger twiddling, and toe twiddling. The finalists then face each other in a twiddle-off.

Talking on the Phone in Your Pajamas and doodling

Athletes compete to see who can talk on the phone the longest while doodling. Scores will be based on doodles, time spent talking, and quality of pajamas.

Making Time to Be Silly in a Busy World, page 22

Silliness is on the rise. Active people find that being silly fits today's more active lifestyle. Listen to what these people are saying about finding time to be silly.

Stockbroker Maggie W. said, "I take time to be silly every day. After a hard day I like to make goofy faces in the mirror. It's great!"

"School is hard," said Chuck C., fourth-grader. "Being silly helps. I put a piece of cheese on my Nose. Then I feel great. Being silly is the best!"

Mona T., mom, claims, "It's important for my kids to learn to be silly when they're young. I want them to be bungling, ridiculous, and doofy. It will help them when they grow up."

"It's hard to find time to act like a fool when you're an important lawyer," explains Bonnie B. "Sometimes during a meeting, I just put my dog on my head and juggle like a clown. Then I take the dog off and continue talking to my client."

Consumer Tips: How to Make Gum Last Longer, page 23

How do I make my gum last longer? That is one of the most frequently asked questions we hear at Consumer Headquarters. After careful study, we've come up with the following helpful tips.

1. Don't chew so much. Studies show that chewing reduces flavor. The more you chew, the more flavor you lose. So try to not chew so much. Just put the gum in your mouth, hold it, and chew once every 60 seconds.

2. Don't chew so hard. Chewing hard reduces flavor. So chew more softly. Imagine you are chewing a tiny robin's egg. Remember that if you chew too hard, you'll break the egg.

3. Take the gum out of your mouth. Spit the gum out in your hand and roll it into a long-lasting ball to make it last forever, donate it to the Museum of Gum.

4. Don't take the gum out of the pack. Gum flavor will last for months if you simply leave it wrapped up in the pack. This is for people who really want long-lasting gum.

5. Don't even buy the gum in the first place. Studies show that the longest-lasting gum of all is gum that you don't buy. After all, if you don't have any gum, how can it lose flavor?

What They Do on Their Day Off, page 24

An interviewed dog said, "By the time I get my day off I'm really exhausted from barking and sniffing all week. I don't bark a bit. If I need to speak, I meow softly. I don't wag my tail, except for emergencies. I lie around and read the newspaper."

Arnie, the couch potato, said, "sitting around watching mindless TV all week is a tough job. On my day off, I avoid television as much as possible. I go to museums. I read a lot. I try to stay away from couches."

A phone interview with a Woman who makes those annoying phone calls selling things revealed, "I love my job. How many people can say that? So on my day off, I spend the day on the phone. I call strangers and ask them if they'd like to change their long distance company. I do this for nothing. That's how much I love my job!"

In the barnyard, a chicken said, "do you know how hard it is to lay an egg every day? On my day off, I like to go horseback riding. Did you say you've never seen a chicken riding a horse? Look around, especially on Tuesdays. A lot of chickens take Tuesdays off for a trail ride."

Answer Key

The Big Interview, page 25

Jerry: Welcome to the show, Ms. Tantrum.

Bobbie: I'd like to say right off that I'm hot under the collar. ~~I'd like to say right off that~~ I'm steaming mad! [and]

Jerry: Why is that?

Bobbie: They ~~is~~ throwing the ball right at my team! [are]

Jerry: Who, Ms. Tantrum? Who's throwing right at you?

Bobbie: The other team! The other team throwing the ball at my team. It isn't right. I'm going to take it anymore! [is] [not]

Jerry: But, coach, this is dodge ball. The point of dodge ball is to throw the ball at the other team.

Bobbie: It is? Who ~~telled~~ you that? [told]

Jerry: It's common knowledge!

Bobbie: Really? No wonder my team never wins.

Jerry: I think that your player Tonya Lightoff has a good arm. Is ~~her~~ your best player? [she]

Bobbie: I guess she can throw ~~hardest~~ than Star Renite. If we play by your rules, Tonya could be the star. ~~His~~ arm is strong. [harder] [Her]

Jerry: What's your game plan, coach?

Bobbie: I think it's time to stop talking and start coaching this team.

Jerry: Thanks, Ms. Tantrum. That ~~were~~ Bobbie Tantrum, coach of the Uptown School dodge ball team. Good night, fans. [was]

The Coming Biscuit Crisis, page 28

The Situation Right Now

At the moment, the biscuit supply holding up. But, biscuits are disappearing at an alarming rate. If this trend keeps up, we be completely out of biscuits by the year 2028. Every day, thousands of biscuit are left uneaten, destroyed, thrown or ~~threw~~ away. Don't let this happen to your biscuits! [is] [will] [thrown]

Trends

Some people seem to think the biscuit supply ~~be~~ endless. It ~~ain't~~. Remember, once you eat a biscuit, it's gone. [is] [isn't]

Organizations

Groups like S.O.B. (Save Our Biscuits) are organizing. They use rallies and concerts to ~~get~~ the word out. Slowly, minds ~~is~~ being changed. People are becoming aware of the Great Biscuit Shortage. [get] [are]

What You Can Do

• Save your biscuits!
• Tell ~~them~~ friends and neighbors to recycle biscuits. [your]
• Organize a Biscuit Day for ~~yours~~ school. [your]

My Most Embarrassing Moment, page 26

Dinah Bingle, Member of Congress, said, "I was giving a speech to the members of the Askalooska Polar Bear Club. Suddenly, I realized that I didn't have any idea what I was talking about! I didn't let that stop me. In fact, I've gone on to become a successful lawmaker. Of course, I still have no idea what I ~~be~~ talking about." [am]

Fred Yerkle, Rude Cab Driver, explained, "I was driving down the street. Suddenly, I noticed that I wasn't snarling, ~~and I noticed that I wasn't~~ being rude, ~~I wasn't~~ changing lanes, tailgating, or hogging the road! I was just driving. I was so embarrassed! Quickly, I went back to my old self and honked at a truck. I felt much ~~more~~ better." [,]

Johnny Pilson, Fourth Grader, said, "I was doing my homework when I realized that the assignment ~~were~~ fun. I didn't ~~told~~ anyone. I thought the feeling would go away. But, it's still here. I actually enjoy doing my homework." [was] [tell]

Louie, a Dog, laughed, "A human spilled something under the table. I think it was a French fry. I didn't run to get it! I don't know what came over me. Maybe it had something to do with that seven-pound turkey leg that I'd just ~~finish~~ eating. Whatever it was, I'm better now. When something spills from the table, I zip over there and grab it!" [finished]

How I Invented the Amazing Spaghetti Gutter, page 29

Take a look at the first picture. That's ~~I~~, Sandy Beech, after eating a bowl of spaghetti. [me]

I love spaghetti. But, spaghetti is a mess! That's why I ~~invent~~ the Amazing Spaghetti Gutter. The Amazing Spaghetti Gutter ~~have~~ patented Total Surround® technology. It works like the cow-catcher on a railroad train to whisk away spills before they pile up! [invented] [has]

Take a look at me after I use the Amazing Spaghetti Gutter. I just ~~ate~~ a big bowl of spaghetti and you can't even tell! My blouse ~~is~~ clean. My chin is dry. The Amazing Spaghetti Gutter sucked up the spills before they even started! [had]

How much would you pay for a 100% all-vinyl Spaghetti Gutter? Millions ~~has~~ been sold for $695.95. But today, in this limited offer, you can order a [have]

Amazing Spaghetti Gutter for only $19.95! That's right! You get the Gutter, attachments, instruction booklet, and video all for only $19.95!

Bonus! If you order today, get 50 ~~feet~~ of extra-heavy duty garden hose for rinsing after a big meal. It's absolutely free! [feet]

Spelling Tips From Mr. Mickey, page 27

Tip 1

Some spelling mistakes ~~is~~ actually correct. For example, the word *wrong* often is spelled wrong. Of course, this ~~be~~ wrong. But it's not a mistake. It's just wrong. [are] [be]

Tip 2

~~Persons~~ often spell words incorrectly when you ask them to lend you money. When they mean to say "yes" they spell their answers "no." [People]

Tip 3

Big words can be tricky. For example, look at the word *diamond.* ~~she~~ may not seem big, there is a mile between the first and last letters of the word. [It]

Tip 4

What's the ~~harder~~ word to spell? That would be *diamond.* A diamond is 13 times harder than steel, and 96 times harder than oatmeal. [hardest]

The following are general tip to improve your spelling.

1. Never spell on a ~~n~~ empty stomach.
2. When spelling dangerous words, always ~~wore~~ a helmet and goggles. [wear]
3. Wash all dirty words with soap and water before ~~spell~~. [spelling]

How to Become a Millionaire Before the Age of 12, page 30

Would you like to be a millionaire before you're twelve? Others have done it. You can do it, ~~to~~. Just follow these helpful pointers. [too]

Step 1 Get to know someone who has several million dollar and want to give some of it away.

Step 2 Ask that person to ~~save~~ you a million dollars. Remember to say, "Please!" [give]

Step 3 If the person ~~don't~~ give you the money, say, "Pretty please with a cherry on top." This ~~usual~~ Works. If it doesn't work, go to step 4. [doesn't] [usually]

Step 4 Beg and whine. If this ~~don't~~ work, go to step 5. [doesn't]

Step 5 Keep your eyes open for the following:
$ Rare coins that ~~be~~ worth a million dollars [are]
$ Buried treasure
$ Big bags of gold
$ Lost art masterpieces
$ Big bags of diamonds

Step 6 If all else fails, become a superstar actor, singer, or athlete. Or, you can just look around for a ~~n~~ big bag stuffed with money.

Scholastic Professional Books *More Proofreading Practice, Please!* Grade 4

Louie's Doggy Dictionary, page 31

Each English entry in Louie's Doggy Dictionary is translated ~~translating~~ into dog language.

ball (bawl) *noun* This is the round thing that you chase. Then, you get food.

down (doun) *verb* This is something that people yell at you. When you hear it, you should jump up several times, then ~~stopped~~ stop. If you don't get any food, try jumping again.

good boy/good girl (gud boi) (gud guhrl) *noun* This means ~~not~~ nothing. It's just something that they say to you before they give you food.

happy (hap • ee) *noun* I am not sure what this word means. I know it has ~~have~~ something to do with food.

hello (hel • oh) *noun* This is ~~am~~ a word that humans use when they want to give you food.

walk (wawk) *noun* This is something you do ~~does~~ around the block before you go home to get food.

Beyond the Microwave, page 32

The Cold Wave

Old-fashioned microwaves make things hot. The Cold Wave makes things cold. Put a spoonful of water in the Cold Wave for 30 seconds and out comes an ice cube!

The Flavor Wave

Suppose you have ~~has~~ a bowl of tasteless mush. Put it in the Flavor Wave for two minutes and it'll bursting with fresh flavor! Leave it in for three minutes and it'll taste like a gourmet meal from an fancy restaurant!

The Reconstituter

Put a chocolate cake in the Reconstituter for six minutes. Soon you get ~~got~~ the ingredients that made the cake: flour, sugar, eggs, chocolate, and milk. How does ~~do~~ this work? We have no idea!

The "Stale-erator"

Do ~~Does~~ you like leftovers? Put fresh food in the "Stale-erator" and turn it on. Soon, it taste four days old! This thing make food so stale no one will want to eat it!

Build a Better Mousetrap Competition, page 33

Virtual Mousetrap

Help the mouse put on a pair of goggles. Inside the goggles, the mouse will see a piece of virtual cheese. When the mouse lunges for the cheese, it gets caught ~~catched~~ in a virtual trap.

Advantage: No muss, no fuss.

Drawback: It works in virtual reality only. In the real world, you're ~~your~~ still stuck with the mouse.

Golf Vacation Get-Away Mousetrap

The mouse is lured by a lavish golf vacation offer. The offer includes transportation, hotel, and golf tiny clubs. The mouse is taken on vacation and ~~and~~ never comes back.

Advantage: Gets rid of the mouse for good.

Drawback: It might ~~maybe~~ attract some human golf fans.

Shop-Till-You-Drop Mousetrap

The mouse is lured by department store sales of up to 80% off. The mouse shop so much that ~~you~~ it finally drops. You haul the mouse away.

Advantage: Gets rid of mouse for good.

Drawback: The mouse will be better dressed than you are ~~is~~.

The Four Biggest Mistakes That Kids Make, page 34

Mistake 1: Leaving a Half-Eaten Candy Bar in Your Room

You start eating a candy bar. Then you put it down. Two years later you find it. Your mom asks, "What's this moldy thing?" You say, "I don't know." She get mad at you. If you don't shape up, she'll ground you. You'll miss the party at Lizett's house.

Mistake 2: Not Finishing Your Homework

You start your homework. Then you get distracted. Your mom asks ~~say~~, "Did you finish your homework?" You say, "No." She threatens to ground you. You may miss the party at Lizett's house.

Mistake 3: Failing to Clean Up Your Room

You start to clean your ~~you're~~ room. Then suddenly you remember that you need to make a phone call. Three hours later, your mom asks ~~say~~, "Why didn't you finish cleaning your room?" You say, "I forgot." Your mom's had enough. You're grounded! You're going to miss the party at Lizett's house.

Mistake 4: Not Remembering the Party

You've been planning for the party all week. Then you do something foolish (like failing to clean up your room). Your mom grounds you! You apologize and promise to correct your mistake. Your mom changes her mind. You hurry to Lizett's house. But you made another mistake. The party is tomorrow!

Behind the Music, page 35

This week we interviewed Harvey Harv about his new ~~its knew~~ song, "Har dee Har."

On the melody and lyrics: Basically, there is no melody. I just hum whatever comes into my head. There are no lyrics. I just sing whatever comes into my head. I know that it doesn't ~~real~~ rhyme or make much sense, but is that necessary for good music?

On those silly hand motions Harvey does when he sings: I imagine I have been tossed in a big vat of vanilla pudding. Then I have to swim to get out. Those hand motions are the way I swim out of the puddin'.

On fans: Fans are cool. I love fans. I'm one of the biggest fans of my fans. In fact, you could say my fans and I are ~~is~~ really alike. Except I'm famous and get paid millions of dollars, and they get nothing.

On fame: I'd rather be known as a good musician than be famous. Wait a minute. No, I wouldn't.

On money: I'd rather be a good musician than have money. Wait a minute. That's not true either. I'd rather have the money.

World Records for Being Late, page 36

Late to School

Bach Nguyen, of river city Iowa, was so late to school that by the time the third-grader showed up to class he was actually in the seventh grade!

Late Library Book

Cicely Petzle of Springfield, Ohio was so late in returning a library book that the library had closed, the building had been torn down, and a bozo Burger restaurant had been built in its place. Cicely ordered a Bozo Burger and fries. Then she sat down and read her overdue book.

Late to Pick Up the Kids at Soccer practice

Sanjay Kota was so late to pick up his daughter at soccer practice that by the time he arrive his daughter had grown up, joined the Olympic soccer team, and won a medal.

Late Homework

Delia Cantu's current events homework report was so late that by the time she turned it in the subject was no longer a current event. In fact, it appeared in Delia's history book in the section called "Voices ~~Voices~~ of the Past."

Answer Key

True Confession: I wore two left shoes for five years!, page 37

It's the truth! I did wore two left shoes for five years. Well, actually it was more like two hours. But it felt like five years!

Here's how it started. I put on my left shoe. Then I put on my other shoe. And, here's the important thing, it be a second left shoe. But, I didn't notice.

At first, it felt funny. I kept thinking, "What's the matter with my shoe?"

Then things got serious. I went to my ballroom dancing class at Hank's house of Dance. My partner, Wanda, said, "Joey, you dance like you've got two left feet!" I thought she was just being critical of my bad dancing. Little did I know.

Finally, we stopped dancing and sat down to get something to drink. I had a root beer. Then Wanda said, "Joey, you're wearing two left shoes."

I looked down. She was right. I was wearing two left shoes. I didn't know what to do.

Did I learn anything from this experience? Yes! Don't wear two left shoes. Don't wear two right shoes, either. If you happen to wear two left shoes, stay calm. Remove the shoe from your right foot. Walk as you would normally. Wearing one left shoe is better than two.

The Evening News, page 40

"For those of you just tuning in, the evening news will now be reported by a new crack team of cat reporters. I'm Richard, and I'm a talking tabby cat. Our top story today is 'Dogs—are they plain no good?' Recent studies have indicated that dogs are loud, stupid, and ugly. But, are they also no good? For more on this breaking story, here's Jennifer."

"This is Jennifer the talking Siamese cat. I'm in the home of a dog named Spot. You'll notice that Spot is sleeping. Let's see what happens when I wake up Spot from his nap."

"BARK! BARK! BARK! BARK! BARK!"

"There you have it, Richard. Just as predicted, this dog was loud, stupid, and, I must say, just plain no good! This is Jennifer reporting live from the home of Spot the dog."

"Thank you, Jennifer. Our next story is 'How delicious is cat food really?' For more on our story, here's Chester."

"Hi, this is Chester the horse. I have six varieties of cat food in front of me. I tasted all of them. Richard, cat food is not delicious!"

"Thank you, Chester. I must say that I disagree with Chester here. I've eaten cat food dozens of times before. I think it's delicious! Well, that's all the time we have now. Join me tomorrow when I'll have a special report 'Is cat nip just for cats?' Until then, good night and good mews, I mean, news."

Science Gab, page 38

DR. FOBES: Hello, I'm Dr. Joann Fobes. Our special guest today on "Science Gab" is Sir Anthony Elwood Burwash Wedge. Sir Anthony is a expert on dog behavior. Let's start by asking the question, "Can dogs talk?" Sir Anthony, can dogs talk?

SIR ANTHONY: I'd like to begin by saying that dogs can talk. I can prove it.

DR. FOBES: How?

SIR ANTHONY: I've taken the liberty of bringing my dog rex to the program. Rex, speak to the nice woman.

REX: Rolf! Yap, yap, yap! Rolf! Yap!

SIR ANTHONY: There. Did you hear that?

DR. FOBES: What did Rex say?

SIR ANTHONY: Wasn't it obvious? He said, "Of course I can talk! Now give me a biscuit!

DR. FOBES: It doesn't sound like that to me. It sounds like yapping and yipping.

SIR ANTHONY: Rex, tell the woman again.

REX: Yap! Rolf, rolf, rolf! Yap! Yap, yap!

SIR ANTHONY: Now, surely you heard that?

DR. FOBES: Heard what?

SIR ANTHONY: I don't think this interview is going well at all. Rex and I are leaving. Say good-bye, Rex!

REX: Yap, yap, yap!

Urban Myths, page 41

Myth 1: There are invisible monsters that eat homework, lose things, and steal your money.

This is absolutely true. Why hasn't anyone ever seen these monsters? You haven't seen them because they're invisible, of course.

Myth 2: Any line you join in the supermarket will end up being the slowest line.

This seems true. But what about the other people? Wouldn't their lines also go the slowest? Doesn't that mean everyone's line would be the slowest? Wait a second. Maybe it is! That explains why it takes so long to shop in the supermarket.

Myth 3: Fast food is neither fast, nor food.

If you don't believe it, order a bucket of chicken. You'll see.

Myth 4: Pigeons are actually intelligent rats who have invented a way to fly.

It's possible. But if they're so intelligent, why are they always begging for food?

Myth 5: If you're nice to others, they'll be nice to you.

This has to be a myth. Hey, wait a minute. Maybe not. Maybe that's the whole problem!

Book Ideas That Failed, page 39

Henry the Snail, Private Detective, by Nancy Noggs
Here are the adventures of Henry the Snail, a private eye who takes him about ten minutes just to answer the phone! By the time he arrives, the case has usually been solved by someone else! Henry uses his wits to make it as a detective.

The Whiners' Club, by Rodney Riter
This book is about a bunch of kids who get together every week to complain about school. They complain about school, finds parents, holes in their socks, you name it!

Why Is Everyone in Fourth Grade Always Looking at Me? by Alice Slack
Main character Annie Dimble goes to school with a big sign on her back that says, STOP STARING AT ME! Of course, everyone stares.

Give Me Back My Ball-Point Pen, by Sonny Day
A boy lends a friend a pen. The book relate the story of his efforts to get the pen back.

Why Is Fourth Grade So Difficult? by Alice Slack
This book is the sixth in the series by Alice Slack, which profiles the life of Annie Dimble. This time, Annie mistakenly enrolls in college instead of the fourth grade. No wonder the homework is so hard!

The Proofreader, page 42

Once there was a proofreader who was very, very lazy. he forgot capitals at the beginnings of sentences. He forgot commas, periods, and other types of punctuation. He even forgot to correct speling erors. Sometimes he even forgot to fix grammar mistakes.

When people told the proofreader about his mistakes, he said, "So what? What could possibly happen from a few proofreading errors?"

One day the proofreader was proofreading a recipe for bagels. The recipe was supposed to call for 14 ounces of yeast. But the proofreader's mistake said 14 pounds of yeast. Well, wouldn't you know it, the proofreader wandered into a bagel store the next day. This was just after the bagel baker had added 14 pounds of yeast instead of 14 ounces.

"I'll have one poppy seed bagel," said the proofreader. Suddenly, the bagels explode. The proofreader got hit by a flying bagel. In fact, it stuck to his nose!

At the hospital, the proofreader asked the doctor, "Why are you laughing?"

"I'm sorry," the doctor said. "I've never seen a bagel stuck to somebody's nose before. How did it happen?"

The proofreader told the story while the doctor extracted the bagel. Today, his nose is as good as new. He's also a much better proofreader. Now he realizes what can happen from just one small mistake.

Scholastic Professional Books More Proofreading Practice, Please! Grade 4